A Baby is a Gift from God

Artwork by

The Land oF MiLk & Honey™

HARVEST HOUSE PUBLISHERS

EUGENE, OREGON

1

A Baby Is a Gift from God

Copyright © 2006 by Harvest House Publishers
Eugene, Oregon 97402
www.harvesthousepublishers.com

ISBN–13: 978-0-7369-1798-8
ISBN–10: 0-7369-1798-5

The Land of Milk and Honey™© 2005 by G Studios, LLC. The Land of Milk and Honey Trademarks owned by G Studios, LLC, Newport Beach, CA USA and used by Harvest House Publishers, Inc., under authorization. For more information regarding art prints featured in this book, please contact:

G Studios, LLC
4500 Campus Drive, Suite 200
Newport Beach, CA 92660
949.261.1300
www.gstudiosllc.com

Design and production by Garborg Design Works, Minneapolis, Minnesota

Harvest House Publishers has made every effort to trace the ownership of all poems and quotes. In the event of a question arising from the use of a poem or quote, we regret any error made and will be pleased to make the necessary correction in future editions of this book.

Unless otherwise indicated, verses are taken from *The Living Bible*, Copyright © 1971. Used by permission of Tyndale House Publishers, Inc., Wheaton, IL 60189 USA. All rights reserved. Verses marked KJV are taken from the King James Version of the Bible.

Printed in China

06 07 08 09 10 11 12 13/ IM / 10 9 8 7 6 5 4 3 2 1

Each child is created in the
special image and likeness
of God for greater things—
to love and be loved.

MOTHER TERESA

Hush, my dear, lie still and slumber.
  Holy angels guard thy bed.
Heavenly blessings without number
  Gently falling on thy head.

ISSAC WATTS *A CRADLE HYMN*

4

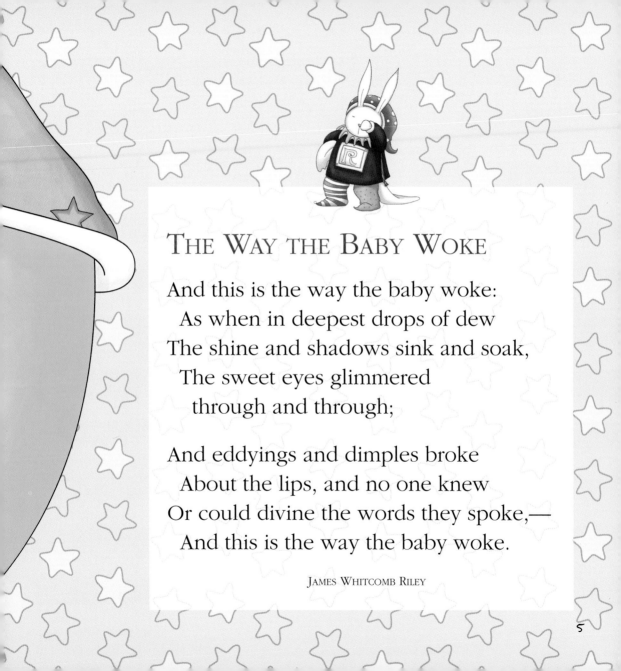

THE WAY THE BABY WOKE

And this is the way the baby woke:
  As when in deepest drops of dew
The shine and shadows sink and soak,
  The sweet eyes glimmered
    through and through;

And eddyings and dimples broke
  About the lips, and no one knew
Or could divine the words they spoke,—
  And this is the way the baby woke.

JAMES WHITCOMB RILEY

5

BABY FEET

Tell me, what is half so sweet
As a baby's tiny feet,
Pink and dainty as can be,
Like a coral from the sea?
Talk of jewels strung in rows,
Gaze upon those little toes,
Fairer than a diadem
With the mother kissing them!
Little feet, so rich with charm,
May you never come to harm.
As I bend and proudly bow
Laughter out of every toe,
This I pray, that God above
Shall protect you with His love,
And shall guide those little feet
Safely down life's broader street.

EDWIN A. GUEST

Fortunately for children,
the uncertainties of the present
always give way to the enchanted
possibilities of the future.

GELSEY KIRKLAND

7

Children are living jewels
dropped unsustained
from heaven.

ROBERT POLLOK

It is a pleasant thing to reflect upon,
and furnishes a complete answer to those
who contend for the gradual degeneration
of the human species, that every baby born
into the world is a finer one than the last.

CHARLES DICKENS

MAKING THE DECISION
TO HAVE A CHILD—IT'S MOMENTOUS.
IT IS TO DECIDE FOREVER TO HAVE YOUR HEART
GO WALKING AROUND OUTSIDE YOUR BODY.

ELIZABETH STONE

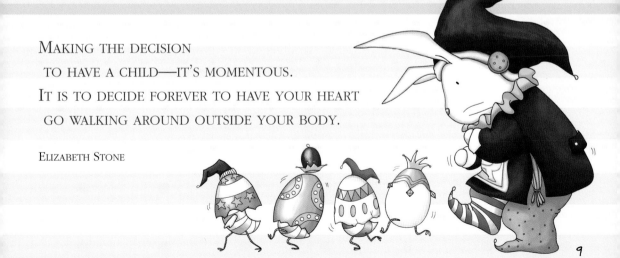

THE BABY

Where did you come from, baby dear?
  Out of the everywhere into the here.
Where did you get your eyes so blue?
  Out of the sky as I came through.
What makes the light in them sparkle and spin?
  Some of the starry spikes left in.
Where did you get that little tear?
  I found it waiting when I got here.
What makes your forehead so smooth and high?
  A soft hand stroked it as I went by.
What makes your cheek like a warm white rose?
  I saw something better than anyone knows.
Whence that three-cornered smile of bliss?
  Three angels gave me at once a kiss.
Where did you get this pearly ear?
  God spoke, and it came out to hear.
Where did you get those arms and hands?
  Love made itself into hooks and bands.
Feet, whence did you come, you darling things?
  From the same box as the cherubs' wings.
How did they all just come to be you?
  God thought about me and so I grew.
But how did you come to us, you dear?
  God thought about you, and so I am here.

GEORGE MACDONALD

10

Bless our children, God, and
help us to fashion their souls by
precept and example that
they may ever honor thy name.

UNION PRAYER BOOK

11

Children are a gift of the LORD...
they are His reward.
Happy is the man who has
his quiver full of them.

The Book of Psalms

For this child I prayed;
and the LORD hath given
me my petition which I
asked of him.

THE BOOK OF 1 SAMUEL (KJV)

Dimpled and flushed and dewy pink he lies,
Crumpled and tossed and lapt in snowy bands;
Aimlessly reaching with his tiny hands,
Lifting in wondering gaze his great blue eyes.

Sweet pouting lips, parted by breathing sighs;
Soft cheeks, warm-tinted as from tropic lands;
Framed with brown hair in shining silken strands,—
All fair, all pure, a sunbeam from the skies!

O perfect innocence! O soul enshrined!

ELAINE GOODALE EASTMAN

Moving between the legs of tables and
of chairs, rising or falling, grasping at
kisses and toys, advancing boldly, sud-
den to take alarm, retreating to the
corner of arm and knee, eager to be
reassured, taking pleasure in the fra-
grant brilliance of the Christmas tree.

T.S. ELIOT

A Little Face

A little face to look at,
A little face to kiss;
Is there anything, I wonder,
That's half so sweet as this?

A little cheek to dimple
When smiles begin
  to grow,
A little mouth betraying
Which way the kisses go.

A slender little ringlet,
A rosy little ear,
A little chin to quiver
When falls the little tear.

A little hand so fragile,
All through the night
  to hold;
Two little feet so tender,
To tuck in from the cold.

Two eyes that watch
  the sunbeam
That with the shadow plays;
A darling little baby,
To kiss and love always.

Author Unknown

17

A BABY IS BORN WITH A NEED TO BE LOVED
AND NEVER OUTGROWS IT.

FRANK A. CLARK

A baby is God's opinion that life should go on. Never will a time come when the most marvelous recent invention is as marvelous as a newborn baby. The finest of our precision watches, the most super-colossal of our supercargo planes don't compare with a newborn baby in the number and ingenuity of coils and springs, in the flow and change of chemical solutions, in timing devises and interrelated parts that are irreplaceable.

CARL SANDBURG

My lovely
living boy,
My hope, my
hap, my love,
my life, my joy.

GUILLAUME DU BARTAS

A new baby is like the beginning of all things—wonder, hope, a dream of possibilities.

EDA J. LeShan

God has plans which mortals don't understand. He rests in the womb when the new baby forms. Whispers the life dream to infinitesimal cells.

ELLEASE SOUTHERLAND

A BABY'S FEET, LIKE SEASHELLS PINK
  MIGHT TEMPT, SHOULD HEAVEN SEE MEET,
AN ANGEL'S LIPS TO KISS, WE THINK,
  A BABY'S FEET.

ALGERNON CHARLES SWINBURNE

21

Children are God's small interpreters.

JOHN GREENLEAF WHITTIER

A woman can learn a lot
from holding a
new baby. It is life
beginning again—
sweet possibilities!
No problem in the world
is big enough to
be remembered.

SUSAN MCOMBER

If there is anything
    that will endure
The eye of God,
    because it is still pure,
It is the spirit of
    a little child,
Fresh from his hand,
    and therefore undefiled.

R.H. STODDARD

A Baby Running Barefoot

When the bare feet of the baby beat across the grass
The little white feet nod like white flowers in the wind,
They poise and run like ripples lapping across the water,
And the sight of their white play among the grass
Is like a robin's song, winsome,
Or as two white butterflies settle in the cup of one flower
For a moment, then away with a flutter of wings.

Long for the baby to wander hither to me
Like a wind-shadow wandering over the water,
So that she can stand on my knee
With her little bare feet in my hands,
Cool like syringa buds,
Firm and silken like pink young peony flowers.

D.H. LAWRENCE

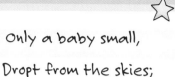

Only a baby small,
Dropt from the skies;
Small, but how dear to us
God knoweth best.

MATTHIAS BARR

A BABY IS...

A baby is cuddles and
   tickles on toes,
the sweet scent of powder,
   a kiss on the nose!
A baby is Teddy bears, rattles,
   and pins,
meals at midnight, giggles,
   and grins.

AUTHOR UNKNOWN

MAY THE HEAVENLY ANGELS
FOLD THEIR WINGS OF WHITE,
O'ER THE SLEEPING CHILDREN
THROUGH THE STARRY NIGHT.

AUTHOR UNKNOWN

26

A babe in
the house is
a well-spring
of pleasure.

PROVERB

A baby is an angel
whose wings decrease
as his legs increase.

MARK TWAIN

THE SWEETEST FLOWERS IN ALL THE WORLD—A BABY'S HANDS.

ALGERNON CHARLES SWINBURNE

They are idols of hearts
  and of households;
They are angels of God
  in disguise;
His sunlight still sleeps
  in their tresses,
His glory still gleams
  in their eyes;
Those truants from home
  and from Heaven
They have made me more
  manly and mild;
And I know now how
  Jesus could liken
The kingdom of God
  to a child.

Charles M. Dickinson

Babies are always
more trouble than
you thought—
and more wonderful.

Charles Osgood

Blessed be the hand that prepares a pleasure for a child, for there is no saying when and where it may bloom forth.

AUTHOR UNKNOWN

The Italian nurse, after taking the baby out in her best, came in with her, and brought her to Anna. The plump, well-fed little baby, on seeing her mother, as she always did, held out her fat little hands, and with a smile on her toothless mouth, began, like a fist with a float, bobbing her fingers up and down the starched folds of her embroidered skirt, making them rustle. It was impossible not to smile, not to kiss the baby, impossible not to hold out a finger for her to clutch, crowing and prancing all over; impossible not to offer her a lip which she sucked into her little mouth by way of a kiss. And all this Anna did, and took her in her arms and made her dance, and kissed her fresh little cheek and bare little elbows; but at the sight of this child it was plainer than ever to her that the feeling she had for her could not be called love in comparison with what she felt for Seryozha. Everything in this baby was charming.

LEO TOLSTOY
ANNA KARENINA

WHEN THE FIRST BABY
LAUGHED FOR THE FIRST TIME,
THE LAUGH BROKE INTO A
THOUSAND PIECES AND THEY
ALL WENT SKIPPING ABOUT...

JAMES M. BARRIE

We can't form our children on our own concepts;
we must take them and love them as God gives them to us.

JOHANN WOLFGANG VON GOETHE